My First
Encyclopedia

Written by **Carol Watson**

London, New York, Munich, Melbourne, and Delhi

Senior Editor Sarah Davis
Senior Designer Victoria Palastanga
Designer Nicola Price
Consultant Ben Morgan
Category Publisher Sue Leonard
Art Director Helen Senior
Publishing Director Mary–Clare Jerram
US Editors Shannon Beatty, Jennifer Quasha
Senior Producer Andrew Beehag
Senior Producer, Pre–Production Tony Phipps

First published in the United States in 1993
Revised edition 2001
This revised edition published in 2013 by
DK Publishing
4th Floor
345 Hudson Street
New York, New York 10014
A Penguin Company

13 14 15 16 10 9 8 7 6 5 4 3 2 1
001—187251—Sep/2013

A catalog record for this book is available from the Library of Congress.

ISBN 978-1-4654-1425-0

Printed and bound in China by Hung Hing

Acknowledgments
With special thanks to the following people:
Chris Bernstein, Dave King, Marie Greenwood, Angela Muss

Picture Credits
The publisher would like to thank the following for their kind permission to reproduce their photographs:
(Key: a-above; b-below/bottom; c-center; f-far; l-left; r-right; t-top)

Alamy Images: David Cook / blueshiftstudios 4clb, 20c, 76br; Paul Fleet,67crb; Melba Photo Agency
48tr,Corbis: Image Source 6bl, 37tc. Dorling Kindersley: Dan Bannister / Rough Guides 69crb; Demetrio
Carrasco /Rough Guides 12fcl; Centaur Studios modelmaker 55tr; Ian Cummings / Rough Guides 54bl; Tim
Draper / Rough Guides 14fcr, 28cl, 65tr, 72fcrb; EddieGerald / Rough Guides 68clb; Edgar Gillingwater -
modelmaker 72ca;Nelson Hancock / Rough Guides 34bl; Jeremy Hunt - modelmaker 50cr; Imperial War
Museum, London 71cla; Diana Jarvis / Rough Guides 29ca; NASA 53tr; National Cycle Collection 37tr;
Natural History Museum, London 2ca (butterfly), 3fcr (butterfly), 6fcra, 6fcr, 6fcrb, 41tc, 62tc, 62ca, 62c
(blue butterfly), 62c (brown butterfly), 63c, 63cb, 63fcr, 78ca, 79ftl (butterfly), 79fcr; Nikid Design Ltd. 34fcl;
Pearson Education 23tc; R. Peterkin / Shutterstock 71crb; Martin Richardson / Rough Guides 29tc; Debbie
Rowe / Pearson Education Ltd. 19br; The Science Museum, London 35cra; Search and Rescue Hovercraft,
Richmond, British Columbia 71ftl; Natascha Sturny / Rough Guides 24bc; Greg Ward / Rough Guides 65tl;
Weymouth Sea Life Centre 51c; Paul Whitfield / Rough Guides 18clb; Jerry Young 66c, 74bc. Dreamstime.
com: James Steidl 54br. Fotolia: dundanim 31tr. Getty Images: Image Source 9br. NASA: KSC 30tr.
PunchStock: Image Source 6fbr, 72ftr.

Jacket images: Front: Dorling Kindersley: NASA cla. Back: Dorling
Kindersley: Jerry Young cl/ (polar bear).

All other images © Dorling Kindersley
For further information see: www.dkimages.com

Discover more at
www.dk.com

My First Encyclopedia

Written by **Carol Watson**

Illustrated by
Mark Ruffle and Ed Myer

A Dorling Kindersley Book

Contents

Notes for parents and teachers

My First Encyclopedia is an exciting and engaging introduction to resource books for preschool children and those that have just started school. With simple text, bold illustrations and beautiful photography, it is not only a useful and creative source of information, but a book that children will enjoy coming back to over time. While a first encyclopedia cannot be comprehensive, it has been specially designed to answer many of the wonderful questions that young people ask about the world as it unfolds around them.

A first book of knowledge

My First Encyclopedia is arranged in a way that parallel's a child's developing curiosity and interests. It covers some of their everyday experiences like going to the doctor and eating healthily, and then branches out to explore themes of the wider world, like science, seasons and weather, and space.

Looking at pictures

The encyclopedia is packed with stunning full-color photography to represent what children see around them. Detailed illustrations show the context in which things are found, and picture sequences reveal some of the processes that occur both in the natural and the human world. When sharing the book with younger children, you can read the text aloud, using the photographs and illustrations as starting points for further discussion. It would be helpful to remind children that not all images are shown to scale.

Reading aloud

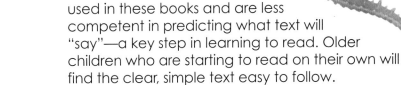

Lots of children have stories read aloud to them, but few experience the same with informational books. As a result, beginning readers are often unfamiliar with the written style used in these books and are less competent in predicting what text will "say"—a key step in learning to read. Older children who are starting to read on their own will find the clear, simple text easy to follow.

Finding information

My First Encyclopedia is designed to help prepare children to find more complicated information in resource books. A complete alphabetical index is included to simplify the task of locating information on specific topics. You can also encourage children to use the index for cross-referencing.

A book to grow up with

In sharing and enjoying this book with your children, you will introduce them to an exciting world of information and knowledge that will be invaluable to them throughout their lives.

Elizabeth Goodacre
Language Consultant

The human body

The human body is made up of different parts, each with a special role to play. All the parts work together so that you can move, breathe, grow, and stay alive.

Skin

Your body is covered all over by layers of skin. The skin protects the inside of your body and stops germs from getting in.

Muscles

Muscles are attached to your skeleton under your skin. You use your muscles for lifting, carrying, and moving around.

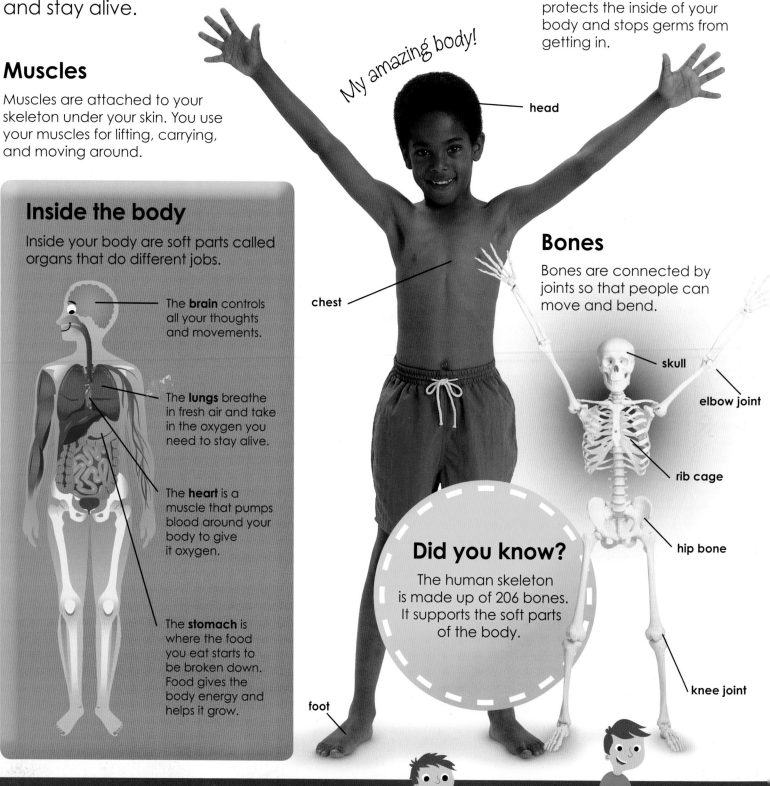

My amazing body!

head

chest

foot

Inside the body

Inside your body are soft parts called organs that do different jobs.

The **brain** controls all your thoughts and movements.

The **lungs** breathe in fresh air and take in the oxygen you need to stay alive.

The **heart** is a muscle that pumps blood around your body to give it oxygen.

The **stomach** is where the food you eat starts to be broken down. Food gives the body energy and helps it grow.

Bones

Bones are connected by joints so that people can move and bend.

skull

elbow joint

rib cage

hip bone

knee joint

Did you know?

The human skeleton is made up of 206 bones. It supports the soft parts of the body.

The Senses

Hearing

You hear with your ears. They collect sounds from the air and send them to your brain. Your brain then tells you what the sounds mean.

Sight

People use their eyes to see. Eyes act like cameras, sending pictures to the brain. Some people need to wear glasses to see clearly.

The Senses

We have five main senses which we use to help our brain gather information about the outside world.

Touch

When you touch something, nerves in your skin send messages to your brain. Your brain can tell whether the thing is soft or hard, rough or smooth, hot or cold.

Taste

Your tongue helps you taste. It is covered with taste buds that can tell if something is sweet or sour, salty or bitter.

Smell

You smell with your nose. Nerves in your nose send messages to your brain, which tells you what you are smelling.

Speech

The vocal cords in your throat make sounds. With your mouth and tongue you can shape the sounds into words so that you can talk.

Twins

All people look a little different. Not even identical twins have exactly the same face.

Growing up

People grow and their bodies change from the minute they are born. People usually stop growing when they are about 20 years old, but their bodies continue to change.

Staying healthy

To stay fit and strong we need to take care of our bodies by keeping clean, eating well, exercising, and getting plenty of sleep. What do you do to stay healthy?

Hair

Hair needs washing, brushing, and combing to keep it strong and shiny.

Sleeping

Sleep gives our bodies and minds a chance to rest. Children need more sleep than adults.

Did you know?

Fingernails grow about twice as fast as toenails! The slowest growing nail on the hand is the thumbnail and the fastest is on the middle finger.

Yum!

Diet

It's important to drink water every day and to eat plenty of fruit and vegetables.

Exercise

We can keep our bodies fit and healthy by exercising often. Exercise makes your muscles stronger.

Brush, brush!

Teeth

When children are about six or seven, their baby teeth fall out and a new set grows. Brushing every morning and night, and not eating too many sweet things help your teeth last a long time.

Visiting the dentist

Teeth and gums are important so we need to get them checked by a dentist. Dentists look for problems, like holes in your teeth, and then fix them.

Keeping clean

Washing all over at least once every day keeps our bodies healthy.

First aid

If you have an accident and cut yourself, an adult will normally act quickly to stop the cut getting infected. This is called first aid. Cuts can be cleaned with warm water and antiseptic and kept clean by covering with a bandage.

Visiting the doctor

Check–up

At a check–up a doctor will make sure that you are developing well by looking at important parts of your body like your eyes, ears, heart, and lungs. A doctor may also give you advice about ways to stay healthy.

Examination

If you are feeling sick a doctor will examine you. Using special instruments like a stethoscope or thermometer the doctor can find out what is wrong and give you medicine if you need it.

Vaccination

Vaccinations stop you from catching serious diseases or getting sick. This little girl is getting a sticker for being brave after her vaccination.

Food and diet

Food helps us grow, gives us energy, and keeps us strong. We get food from animals and plants and turn it into different meals. Some food can be eaten raw, but other food tastes better when it is cooked.

Food groups

The five main food groups for a balanced diet are shown here. They are shown in roughly the right proportions. Getting the balance of food right every day is important, but you don't need to do it at every meal.

World foods

Sashimi
Sashimi is a popular Japanese dish of fresh, raw meat or fish.

Curry
Popular in India, this meat or vegetable dish is made with special spices and served with rice.

Pizza
This bread–based meal, topped with tomato sauce and cheese, comes from Italy.

Fats and sugars

Fats from food like butter and bacon give the body energy for growth, but we need to make sure we eat the right amount since too much fat can be bad for us.

Meat can be cooked in many different ways. It can be fried, roasted, or grilled in an oven or on a barbecue.

Starch

Potatoes, bread, cereal, rice, and pasta are all starchy foods. These foods give us energy.

Bread is a popular food everywhere.

Many people eat **rice** as an everyday staple.

Protein

Cheese, meat, eggs, nuts, and fish give us protein that helps us grow. Most fish and meat needs to be cooked before eating. Vegetarians are people that choose not to eat meat.

Fiber

Fruit and vegetables have plenty of fiber. They help the food that you eat to pass through your body.

Tomatoes have become an important ingredient in many different types of cuisine, adding color, juice and flavor.

Vegetables can be squeezed in a blender to make vegetable juice. Try making one yourself! Which combinations make the best flavor?

Countries all over the world make **cheese**, with flavors and textures specific to their region.

Drinks

We need to drink water every day. Fruit juice is another tasty cold drink, and hot drinks full of milk are delicious on cold days.

Fruit is full of vitamins and makes a great healthy snack.

Dairy

Dairy products like milk, cheese, and yogurt contain calcium, which help our bones grow strong.

Did you know?

The amount of dairy food that people eat varies from country to country. In some parts of the world people do not eat this food group at all—it makes them feel unwell.

Growing food

Much of our food comes from crops grown by farmers all over the world. Some farmers grow plants like cereals in open fields. Others grow vegetables and fruit in greenhouses.

Cereal

Cereals are grasses that are grown for their seeds. The seeds are called grain. Grain is used to make flour for foods like bread and pasta.

oats

rye

wheat

barley

Sugar cane

Sugar cane is a giant grass that grows in hot countries. The thick stem is called cane and is full of sweet juice. The juice is used to make sugar.

Sunflower

Sunflowers produce hundreds of seeds. The seeds are squeezed to give us oil for cooking.

Rice

Rice is grown in fields flooded with water, called paddies. Above, rice farmers have cut big steps, or terraces, into steep hillsides to make flat paddy fields.

Sowing

Farmers plow their fields with tractors before they plant the grain seeds.

Ripening

The seeds grow into plants. New seeds grow on the plants and ripen in the sun.

Harvesting

The farmers use combine harvesters to separate the ripe grain from the stems.

I love growing my own food!

Salad vegetables

In cold regions lettuce, cucumbers, tomatoes, and other salad vegetables are grown in greenhouses to protect them from cold weather.

Growing fruit

Some fruit—like bananas—grow in hot countries. Others, like apples and oranges, grow on trees in orchards. Grapes grow on vines in vineyards and are used to make juice or wine.

Green vegetables

Cabbage, cauliflower, and broccoli are grown in fields. They grow well in places that have a lot of rain.

Root vegetables

Some plants have tasty roots that we can eat. Potatoes, beets, parsnips, and carrots are all root vegetables.

Did you know?

Tomatoes are a fruit even though we think of them as a vegetable.

Pod vegetables

Vegetables like peas and beans are seeds that grow inside the seed pod of a plant. They are picked out of the pod and frozen, canned, dried, or eaten fresh.

Grow your own

Step 1
Plant some seeds.

An empty egg box is great for planting seeds. Use good rich soil or a compost–based soil. Peas, radishes, and tomatoes are good seed choices. They will sprout quickly.

Step 2
Water them regularly.

It is important to make sure you keep the soil well watered but not waterlogged.

Step 3
Watch them grow.

tomato plants

Family

A family is a group of people who are related to each other. Some are small, some are large, and they are all different. In some families just one parent lives with the children, in others there are two. Sometimes grandparents live in the family home too.

Mom's side of the family

Grandparents

Aunt

Uncle

Mom

Cousin

Me and my family!

Aunt
If your mother or father has a sister, she is your aunt. Your aunt's husband is also your uncle.

Uncle
If your mother or father has a brother, he is your uncle. His wife is your aunt.

Parents
Your mother and father are your parents.

Cousin
If your aunt and uncle have children, they are your cousins.

Did you know?
If a child can't be taken care of by his or her own family, he or she can be adopted and live permanently with another family.

Dad's side of the family

Grandparents

Grandparents

Your grandparents are your mother and father's parents. You are their grandchild.

Dad

Aunt

Uncle

Brother

Sister

Cousin

Stepfamily

Stepfamilies are created when an adult—who already has children—marries, or lives with someone again. This can happen after a partner dies, but is common after the breakdown of a relationship.

Marriages

Some people decide to get married and make a commitment to this special relationship. Their families often get together with friends to celebrate the day.

Birthdays

Each year we all have a birthday. Some people celebrate with parties, inviting friends and family to join them, eating, and playing games together.

New family members

When new babies are born, families change and everyone has to readjust. Taking care of a new baby is lots of fun but also very tiring.

Houses and homes

There are many different ways to live. Some people live in a house or apartment. People called nomads move around, living in tents or vehicles. Some homes are large with many rooms with different uses, others are smaller with one or two rooms.

A **"high–rise"** is made up of many small homes or apartments built on top of one another. They are common in crowded cities.

apartment building

townhouses

high–rise apartment building

Types of home

Homes come in all shapes and sizes— from houses and cottages built with wood, bricks, or stone, to modern apartments made of glass and concrete.

wooden house

brick house

stone house

An RV, or recreational vehicle like this one, is a home on wheels. People can drive to and stay in various places.

Attic

Attic space under the roof of a house is useful for keeping things in that you don't use regularly.

Bathroom

There is usually a bathtub or shower, a sink, and a toilet in a bathroom. Washing and brushing teeth is done here.

Living room

A living room is a comfortable room where people can read, relax, or watch television.

Study

Some houses have a study, which is useful for doing homework in.

Bedroom

Bedrooms are a private space for sleeping, relaxing, and often, for playing. Some people share bedrooms.

Kitchen

People use a kitchen to store, prepare, and cook their food. Most modern homes have gas or electric stoves for cooking.

House on stilts

Stilts can make a house level when it is built on a steep hillside.

People who live near rivers and marshes often build their homes on stilts. The stilts keep the house high up off the ground, protecting it from floods.

Igloo

Igloos are made of blocks of snow and are the traditional homes of the Inuit people. Today, it is more common for people who live in cold areas to live in modern homes made of wood, bricks, or concrete.

Houseboat

A houseboat is a home that floats on water. Some people live on their houseboats all the time.

Pets

Many people keep animals as pets. They are fun to play with and feed, but taking care of them is also hard work. Two of the most common pets are cats and dogs.

Dog

Dogs come in all shapes, sizes, and breeds. They are very intelligent and quick to learn, which means they have become important in communities as well as as companions.

Fish

Pet fish are kept in glass tanks called aquariums. They are fascinating to watch as they swim around. Goldfish are the most popular breed of pet fish. They need to be fed every day.

Guinea pig

Guinea pigs are very social animals and love living with other guinea pigs. Their teeth are constantly growing so they need things to chew to keep them worn down.

Rabbit

Rabbits are naturally shy animals, but if you play with them often they quickly become tame. They can be kept indoors or outdoors but they need plenty of space to run around.

I sleep all day and prowl around at night!

Cat

Cats enjoy playing and being stroked, but they also need time by themselves. After a meal, a cat will often spend time washing itself.

A bed
Dogs can sleep indoors in a dog bed or outdoors in a kennel.

Pet care
Pets need care and attention to keep them healthy, happy, and safe. It is important to find out all about an animal before deciding whether it is a good match for you or your family.

Exercise
Most dogs need plenty of exercise, and love going on long walks.

Playing
Many dogs love playing with balls, sticks, and dog toys.

I like bones!

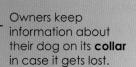

Owners keep information about their dog on its **collar** in case it gets lost.

Feeding
Dogs need fresh food and water every day.

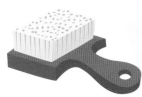

Care
Brushing a dog's coat regularly keeps it in good condition.

Visiting the vet

Sick pet

If your pet is sick, stops eating, or drinks more than usual, it should be taken to the vet.

Check-up

The vet will examine your pet and look for signs of illness or upset.

Medicine

Your pet might need pills or special food to help it get better. It might have to stay at the vet's overnight.

People at play

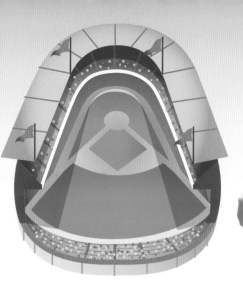

We play sports for fun, to relax or for exercise. Some sports are played on your own, others are played by groups of people in teams.

Yoga

In a yoga class a teacher demonstrates different positions to do in order to stretch and strengthen muscles and improve flexibility. Breathing and relaxation techniques are also an important part of the class.

Did you know?

Soccer is one of the most popular sports in the world. Every four years the World Cup tournament is watched on television by billions of people all over the globe.

Watching sports

People go to large sports stadiums to watch their favorite sports or teams in action.

soccer ball

Dancing

There are many types of dance, from ballet and hip hop, to line and ballroom. Making up a dance of your own is really fun too!

Running

Many people enjoy running, for fun or in races. They run on roads or tracks, both indoors and outdoors.

Runners wear **sneakers** with thick, soft soles to protect and support their feet.

Basketball

Basketball is played by two teams of 10 players each. Five players from each team work together to score points. A team scores points when a player throws the ball into the basket.

This gymnast is wearing a stretchy leotard so she can move easily.

Gymnastics

Gymnasts need to be strong and supple in order to be able to jump, somersault, balance, twist, and cartwheel.

Ball games

Many sports are played with a ball. Can you match the ball to the correct piece of equipment and guess the game?

A

B

C

D

E

1

2

3

4

5

ANSWERS: 1B—Football, 2C—Baseball, 3E—Golf, 4A—Tennis, 5D—Cricket.

Clothes

Clothes come in all shapes, sizes, colors, and materials. They keep us warm when it's cold, and cool when it is warm. We have different clothes for day, night, special occasions, sports, and fun. People from all over the world wear different types of clothes.

Cold places

People who live in very cold countries, like Tibet, wear lots of thick layers of clothing made from fur, wool, or felt.

Hot places

In very hot countries, like Egypt, people often wear long, flowing robes made from white cotton to keep cool.

Festivals

Some festivals are celebrated by dressing up in brightly colored clothes. This Japanese girl is wearing a robe called a yukata to celebrate a summer festival.

A **sari** is an Indian dress made from a single piece of fabric.

Did you know?

Clogs are shoes made partly or completely from wood. They come from Europe where they were originally worn by workers as protective footwear.

Can you pick what you would like to wear today? Don't forget to look at the weather.

Protective clothing

Some clothes are used to protect our bodies and keep us safe, like sports helmets and life jackets. Others stop us from getting dirty, and some protect us from the weather.

Bicycle helmet

Sun hat

Apron

Life jacket

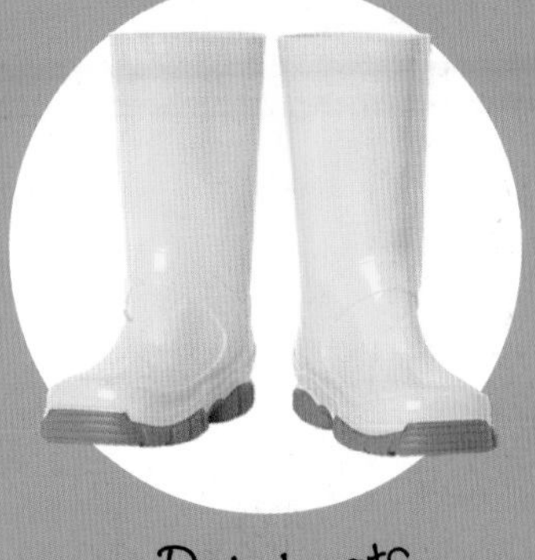

Rain boots

Dress up

Dressing up for celebrations like Halloween, carnivals, or just at home, is fun! Who would you most like to dress up as?

Uniforms

People wear uniforms to show that they belong to a certain group or do the same job. Some children also wear a uniform to school.

25

Action!

Jobs

Most people work to earn money to pay for a home, food, and clothes. Some jobs —like being a doctor—take years of studying, and others are best learned as they are practiced.

Cook

Cooks prepare and make food in restaurants, schools, cafes, and other businesses. Chefs are cooks who have a qualification in food preparation and more experience of the food industry as a whole.

Doctor

Doctors listen to people talk about their health issues, do tests to see what is wrong, and give advice about staying well. They also send patients to other specialist doctors if they need specific care.

Movie director

A movie director is the person who directs the actors and film crew when making a movie. They also work on the overall look of the movie.

Jobs in a car factory
Factories provide many jobs for people with lots of different skills.

Designer
The designer thinks up ideas for how a car will look and makes detailed drawings of each part.

Machine operator
The machine operator controls the machines that cut out the metal parts of the car and weld them together.

Assembly–line worker
Assembly–line workers work in a team to put together, or assemble, all the different parts of each car.

School teacher

A school teacher provides an education for children, and usually has a professional qualification. Teachers can teach a specific subject or teach about many topics.

Did you know?

Firefighters used to be called "bucket brigades" because fires were originally put out by people passing water in buckets down a line to extinguish them.

Going to school

Going to school every day and working hard is a good way to learn about what job you might like to do when you are older.

Farmer

Being a farmer is hard work! But it is also an important job all over the world. Farmers make a living by selling their plants, animals, and animal products.

Firefighter

Firefighters put out fires, which is not as simple as it may sound. Fighting fires is dangerous and complex, and it takes organization and teamwork.

Supervisor

The supervisor makes sure that the assembly-line workers are doing their jobs well.

Quality tester

The quality tester checks the finished car and makes sure that everything is working correctly.

Driver

The driver's job is to drive the car transporter, loaded with new cars, to the place where they will be sold.

Towns and cities

Towns and cities are busy places where millions of people live and work. Big towns are filled with buildings, from places of worship, to offices and stores. People gather in towns and cities to see each other, go out, visit places of interest, live, and work.

Cities

A city is a large town with a greater population of people. Because of its size it is run by larger and more powerful organizations than a town. Here are some of the biggest and busiest cities in the world.

Tokyo, Japan

Seoul, South Korea

Mexico City, Mexico

New York City, USA

Office building

An office building is often built in the middle of a crowded city. Lots of businesses can have their office in one building.

Building site

In most cities, there are building sites where new stores, houses, and offices are being built. Builders use special machinery and trucks to get the buildings ready.

Park

Parks are natural green spaces where city people can escape from the crowded streets and noisy traffic.

School

There are often schools and colleges in a town or city. School buildings look different depending on what kind of school it is.

Movie theater

It's fun to go to the movies with friends. Some movie theaters are huge and can play lots of movies at the same time.

Park

School

Building site

Movie Theater

Places of worship

There are six major religions in the world. Each one has a special building where members can worship.

Christian church

Hindu temple

Buddhist temple

Muslim mosque

Jewish synagogue

Sikh gurdwara

Town hall

In most towns, there is a town hall. The people who manage the town work here. There are also large rooms for meetings and special events.

Hospital

A hospital is a place where sick and injured people go to be cared for. Nurses and doctors look after them and try to make them well again. People often go to hospital in an ambulance.

Factory

Factories are often built on the outskirts of a town. This means that trucks delivering to the factories do not have to drive through the heavy traffic in the city center.

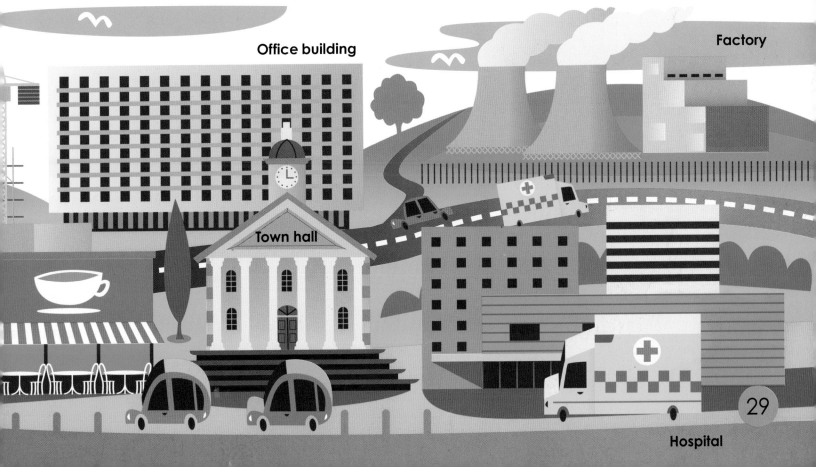

Office building

Factory

Town hall

Hospital

What is science?

Science is a way of asking questions and testing ideas in order to find out more about the universe, our Earth and everything in it, including you! There are many different types of science. Here are some of the things that scientists study in order to try and work out how the universe works.

Space

Some scientists are involved in examining space and all things in it, including the Sun, stars, and planets. This part, or branch, of science is called astonomy.

Life

Scientists study all living things —plants, animals, even your own body. They ask questions about how living things work, grow, and survive. Biology is the branch of science that studies life.

I love learning about wildlife!

Matter

All the things on and around you— your clothes, toys, books, even the hairs on your head—are broken down into matter. Chemistry and physics are the parts of science that look at matter.

Did you know?

Helium is a gas that is lighter than air—making it perfect for the special balloons you sometimes get at parties.

Forces

A force pulls or pushes something, making it move or keeping it in place. Magnets have a force that attracts or repels (pushes away) other metals. Gravity is a very important type of force. Without it, you would fly off into space! Physics looks at both force and energy.

Earth

Planet Earth is special. It is the only place in the universe, as far as is known, where there is life. Geologists study how the Earth was made and what it is made of.

Atoms

Everything in the universe is made up of tiny particles called atoms. Atoms are so small you can't see them, and yet they are a vital part of scientific study.

Types of energy

Electricity

Heat

Light

Sound

Movement

Energy

Although we can't see it, energy is all around us. When we turn the lights on we are using energy, when we use the car, it is burning energy, and when we get out of bed it is our own energy that gets used up. It is the substance that makes things happen.

Being a scientist

There are lots of different types of scientist, and some of them are shown on these pages. They each have specialist areas of expertise but they all test out ideas to try to fill in gaps in our knowledge.

Testing time

Scientists do tests, called experiments, to try and prove their ideas or theories about the world.

test tubes

hair tied back

goggles

funnel-shaped flask

white coat

Did you know?

When water freezes and becomes ice it expands (gets bigger). This is why freezing water can cause water pipes to burst.

magnifying glass

Safety first

Scientists often wear special clothing like a white coat and goggles when doing an experiment. This is to protect them from possible harm from chemicals.

microscope

Up close

Scientists use microscopes and magnifying glasses to magnify (make bigger) tiny things that you can't see with the naked eye.

Thirsty flower

This experiment shows how a flower collects water and food from the soil and sucks them up into its stem. Try it out! But don't forget to ask an adult to help.

Step 1
Cut the end of a flower stem at an angle and place it in a glass of water.

Step 2
Add a few drops of food coloring to the water. Leave it for up to 24 hours.

Step 3
Take a look at the flower now! The stem has sucked up the water like a straw and the petals have turned red.

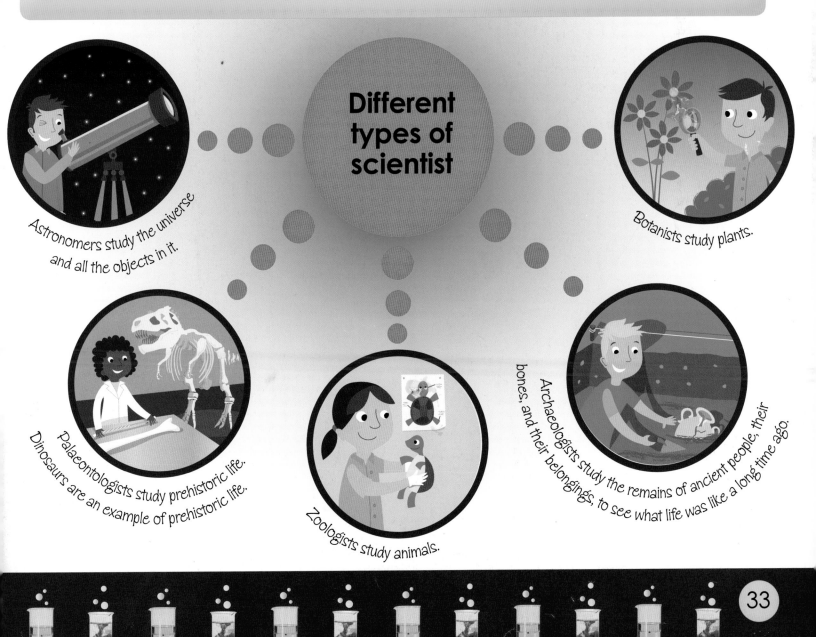

Different types of scientist

Astronomers study the universe and all the objects in it.

Botanists study plants.

Palaeontologists study prehistoric life. Dinosaurs are an example of prehistoric life.

Zoologists study animals.

Archaeologists study the remains of ancient people, their bones, and their belongings, to see what life was like a long time ago.

I use my laptop to talk to friends!

Science all around

Scientists are constantly making new discoveries and inventing new things to help make our lives easier and safer. This practical use of inventions in everyday life is known as technology. Here are some of the ways that technology has helped improve our lives.

Electricity

Electricity travels along wires as a current, carrying energy. The energy is used to make heat, light, sound, and movement. Many of the machines we use in our daily lives are powered by electricity.

iron

washing machine

blender

Times Square in New York is flooded with lights powered by **electricity**.

Communications

Today all kind of technological devices are around that help make communications easier and faster. We use email and the Internet and can text or call people on our mobile phones. We can even record or download television programs and watch them whenever we want.

I can listen to music without disturbing you.

headphones

5:35

whoosh!

bullet train

Medicine

Thanks to science and technology, many illnesses that used to be untreatable can now be prevented or cured.

Today, surgeons use the latest **technology** to perform complicated operations that can save lives.

Satellite

Satellites have transformed the way we communicate with each other and send information around the globe—instantly.

How satellites work

Satellites are a bit like giant mirrors in the way they bounce television pictures, telephone calls, and internet signals from one side of Earth to the other.

The satellite dish sends the signals to a satellite high up in space.

Radio signals are beamed from a satellite dish.

Signals are sent back down to Earth.

The cameraman films the soccer player.

The soccer player appears on your television!

Great inventions

Inventions are new things designed by people, often to make life better—whether it be improving health or making life more comfortable in some way. People have been inventing things for thousands of years. Everything was invented by someone, from the bristles in your toothbrush to the latest mobile phone.

Be an inventor for the day! Draw pictures of new things you would like to create.

Telescope

We use telescopes to study the night sky—to see stars and planets in more detail. The first telescopes were invented by three craftsmen from the Netherlands, who also made spectacles (glasses).

1600s

Computer

The first electronic digital computers were developed between 1940 and 1945. Originally, they were the size of a large room, using as much power as several hundred modern computers. They looked very different to today's laptops, like the one below.

1900s

Did you know?

The wheel is one of the oldest and most important inventions. But nobody is quite sure who invented it.

Steam engine

The earliest steam engines were built more than 300 years ago. Wood or coal was burned to heat up water. Then the steam from the water would power the engine. Early steam engines powered trains and ships.

1700s

1800s

Light bulb

From the 1800s, inventors were eager to make electricity produce light. The first light bulbs only lasted a few minutes. But over time they were improved to last much longer.

1800s

Bicycle

The first practical two-wheeled vehicle was the German draisine dating back to 1817. It had no pedals, so the person riding it had to use their feet to push it along.

Television

Scottish engineer John Logie Baird produced the first television pictures. Early televisions were huge compared to today and only showed black and white pictures. Color television started to become popular in the 1960s.

1900s

1800s

1800s

Telephone

The invention of the telephone meant that people all over the world could talk to each other. With the invention of the mobile phone, we now carry our phones around with us.

Camera

Cameras capture our favorite moments and record them so we can show family and friends. The first cameras looked like wooden boxes and took hours to take one photo. Today, many people own digital cameras and have cameras on their phones.

Plants

There are millions of plants in the world. We use them for food, to make clothes, and as medicine. A plant is made up of a stem with leaves and flowers, and roots that grow under the ground.

Flowers are the part of a plant that makes **seeds**.

Leaves grow from the plant's **stem**.

Flowers

Many plants have flowers on their stems. People grow flowering plants, like roses, because of their look and smell. Some flowers, like the blossoms on apple trees, turn into fruit that we eat.

Herbs

Herbs are useful plants. They can be used to make natural medicines or chopped up and cooked to flavor food. Some herbs are crushed and their oils are used to make perfume.

bluebell

mint

lavender

parsley

Roots take water from the soil.

Seeds and bulbs

When a flower dies, it leaves behind a seed head filled with tiny seeds. The seeds drop to the ground and grow into new plants. Some plants, like daffodils, grow from bulbs as well as seeds. Some bulbs grow a new part every year, which forms a new plant.

seed head

The **seed head** is the part in the middle.

seed pod

seeds in pod

bulb

Potted plants

Some people decorate their homes with plants grown in pots. Most potted plants grow best in a room with plenty of sunlight. Potted plants also need to be watered to stay healthy.

People often choose potted plants with colorful or patterned leaves to grow in their homes.

Garden

Some people have their own gardens where they can grow their favorite plants. They dig flower beds and spend time weeding, watering, and caring for them.

My first potted plant!

Window box

Many people grow flowers and plants in narrow boxes. They put the boxes on a windowsill in the sun. The plants grow well in the warmth and light, but they need plenty of water.

Did you know?

Wild flowers grow by themselves. Their seeds are carried by the wind or by animals. When the seeds reach the ground, they grow into new plants.

Planting

Flower seeds are planted in holes in the ground. Then the seeds are covered with soil and watered well.

Sprouting

As the ground is warmed by the sun, the seeds begin to sprout. Shoots appear above the ground and roots grow into the soil.

Flowering

Leaves begin to grow from the shoots. As the plant grows taller, buds appear. The buds swell open into flowers.

Bugs and insects

Tiny creatures live all around us—both indoors and outside. There are thousands of different types—from flying insects, like bees and flies, to climbing spiders and snails that crawl along the ground.

Dragonfly

These expert flying machines cannot walk—despite having six legs—but can fly up to 40 mph (about 64 kph). They have been around since before the dinosaurs.

Ladybug

A ladybug is a small beetle. It has dark spots on its brightly colored wing cases. Ladybugs eat smaller insects.

Bee

Bees live in a group called a colony. Each colony has one queen bee who lays the eggs. Worker bees collect sweet juices from flowers to make honey.

When bees fly, the flapping of their wings makes a buzzing sound.

BUZZZZZZZZZZ!!!!

On the ground

Hundreds of bugs and insects live beneath our feet. Ants and beetles scurry along looking for food, slugs glide slowly through the grass, and worms burrow into the earth.

leaf butterfly

Did you know?

Some insects, like the leaf butterfly and stick insect, match their surroundings. This helps them hide from enemies. It is called being camouflaged.

stick insect

Butterfly life cycle

Caterpillar

A female butterfly lays eggs on a plant. The eggs hatch out into caterpillars, which eat the plant's leaves.

Spider

All spiders have eight legs. They catch and eat small flying insects, like flies and moths. A spider kills its prey with a poisonous bite.

Chrysalis

Each caterpillar grows big and fat. Its skin hardens and it turns into a chrysalis, or pupa.

spider web

Most spiders spin a sticky web between the branches of trees or bushes. Spiders lie in wait to catch insects that fly into their webs.

Fly

Like most insects, flies have six legs. They have only one pair of wings. Flies can flap their wings so fast that they seem to stay still in the air.

Snail

A snail glides along the ground on one large foot, leaving a trail of slime behind it. In times of danger it can hide its soft body inside the hard shell on its back.

Butterfly

After a few weeks, the pupa splits. A butterfly climbs out. When its wings dry, it flies away.

Earthworm

Earthworms help keep the soil healthy by making holes that let air and water into the ground.

A snail's eyes are on the end of its feelers.

feelers

Trees

A tree is a tall plant with a wood stem called a trunk. Trees are the largest living things in the world and can live for hundreds of years. A large group of trees growing together is called a forest.

Fruit and seeds

Many trees produce fruit of some kind. The fruit drops from the tree and is scattered by the wind or carried away by animals. Inside the fruit are seeds. If they reach the soil they can grow into new, young trees.

acorn

chestnut

peach   pinecone

Tree

Trees with leaves that turn brown and drop off in the fall are called deciduous trees. Trees with narrow leaves that stay green on the tree all year round are called conifers or evergreens.

deciduous tree   conifer

Leaf

There are two kinds of leaves. Thin, waxy leaves called needles grow on conifers. Broad leaves grow on deciduous trees. These can be simple leaves, or compound leaves made up of lots of leaflets growing from one stem.

compound leaf

simple leaf

pine needles

Tree trunk

Every year, a tree trunk grows another layer of wood, which makes a ring. People can count the rings to find out how many years the tree has been alive.

This is a sideways slice of a tree's trunk, showing its rings.

Tree house

A tree is home to all sorts of creatures. Birds roost and nest in the branches. Squirrels run up and down the tree trunk and make leafy nests called dreys. Insects buzz around in the treetops or scuttle about among the roots.

trunk

Natural forest

For thousands of years, trees have grown naturally in forests all over the world. Trees are very important because they give off oxygen that all animals, including humans, need to breathe.

Fewer trees need to be cut down if old paper is recycled and used to make new paper.

Things made from wood

Many useful things are made from wood.

Chair
Wooden planks are used for building or making furniture like chairs.

Paper
Wood chips are crushed into pulp to make paper.

branch

leaves

Timber

Some trees are gown especially for their wood, or timber. When the trees are big enough, they are chopped down. The trunks, or logs, are taken to a saw mill where they are cut into flat strips, called planks.

Bark is the tree's skin. It protects it from insects and diseases.

Did you know?

Wild rabbits live in holes in the ground called warrens or burrows. The entrance to a rabbit warren is often hidden in the roots of a tall tree.

Birds

Birds are the only animals that have feathers. All birds have wings, but not all of them can fly. Some birds live together in large groups called flocks, while others live alone.

Parakeet

Brightly colored parakeets are naturally found in tropical rain forests. They use their strong, hooked beaks to crack open the seeds and nuts that they eat.

Falcon

A falcon is a bird of prey. It uses its sharp beak and claws to catch and eat small animals.

A duck dips its beak into the water to find insects, worms, and plants to eat.

Flight

Most birds have perfect bodies for flying. Their hollow bones are light and very strong. Birds fly by flapping their wings or by gliding on currents of air. Some birds can flap their wings so fast that they can hover in the air.

Duck

Ducks live near ponds and rivers. The toes on their feet are joined with flaps of skin. They use these webbed feet as paddles to swim.

Feathers

A bird has different kinds of feathers. Tail and wing feathers help the bird fly. The outer feathers are special colors to hide the bird from its enemies or help the bird show off to its mate. Soft down feathers grow close to the bird's body to keep it warm.

Did you know?

The world's tallest and heaviest living bird is the ostrich. It cannot fly but with its long, strong legs it can run incredibly fast on land.

body feather

down feather

tail feather

Feeding

Many wild birds feed on berries, insects, and seeds. Some people put seeds, bread, and nuts in feeders for birds to eat.

Pelican

Pelicans live on riverbanks and by the seashore. A pelican's beak has a stretchy pouch, which it uses like a fishing net to scoop up fish to eat.

Kiwi

A kiwi's wings are so small that it cannot fly. Common in New Zealand, it lives and nests on the ground and hunts at night. It uses the nostrils at the end of its beak to sniff out food in the dark.

Flamingo

Flamingos live together in big flocks beside lakes and marshes. They wade through the water on their long legs.

Breeding

Laying

Female birds lay eggs, often in a nest built high in a tree. The female or male bird sits on the eggs to keep them warm.

Hatching

When a baby bird, or chick, hatches from the egg, its eyes are usually closed. Many chicks have no feathers.

Growing

The mother and father fly back and forth with food for the chicks. When the chicks' feathers grow, they can fly and feed themselves.

Farm animals

Many kinds of animals are kept on farms. We get milk, eggs, and wool from the animals. Some are killed for their meat. It is the farmer's job to feed and care for the animals.

Dairy food

One cow can produce up to 3 gal (about 14 liters) of milk a day. The milk can be turned into products like yogurt, cheese, and butter.

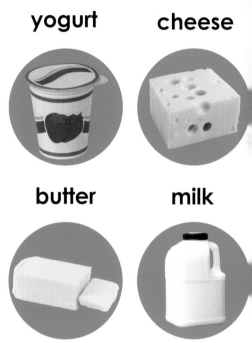

yogurt

cheese

butter

milk

Baby pigs are piglets.

Pig

Pigs are kept for their meat, which is called pork. Pigs live in sties and eat vegetables and cereal. A female pig is called a sow. She can have more than 15 piglets at a time!

Goat

Goats are good climbers and can live on steep hillsides. Farmers keep goats for their milk, which is turned into cheese. A female goat is called a nanny goat and a young male goat is a buck.

Sheepdog

The sheepdog's job is to help the farmer round up the sheep in the fields. The farmer calls and whistles to the dog to tell it what to do.

A baby goat is a kid.

Did you know?

Many people think that pigs are dirty because they are always covered in mud. Actually they roll around in mud to keep themselves cool.

oink, oink!

woof, woof!

Wool farming

Rounding up
In the spring, farmers and their dogs round up the sheep, ready to be sheared. They have grown thick coats during the winter.

Shearing
Farmers shear the sheep, cutting off their fleece. The fleece is spun into wool.

Warm clothes
The wool is dyed and made into different types of clothes like sweaters and hats.

Cattle

Cattle are kept for their meat, which is called beef. Cattle live in large groups called herds. They graze on open grasslands on big farms called ranches or stations.

Bulls, steers, and **oxen** are male cattle.

Chicken

Female chickens are called hens. A hen lays an egg nearly every day. Farmers collect the eggs and sell them to stores where we can buy them.

Sheep

Sheep live together in groups called flocks. They graze on grass in fields or paddocks. A ewe is a female sheep and a ram is a male sheep.

Cow

Female cattle are called cows. Farmers keep cows for their milk. Cows live in herds and graze in fields. They need to be milked every day.

A baby chicken is a chick.

A baby sheep is a lamb.

A baby cow or bull is a calf.

cheep, cheep!

baa, baa!

moo, moo!

47

Seashore

The seashore is the place where the land meets the sea. Colorful shells and seaweed are washed up on to the beaches, and tide pools teem with curious sea life like starfish and sea anemones. It's a great place to play and explore!

Shell

Many kinds of shell can be found on the beach. Shells are the home of sea creatures. People collect empty shells with bright colors or interesting shapes.

whelk

tower shell

scallop

cone shell

Sting winkle

top shell

Starfish

These sea animals have a spiny skin. They are not fish and cannot swim, but instead, use the suckers under their five arms to help them climb over rocks under the water.

Crabs

Crabs have 10 legs. They use eight legs to swim and scuttle sideways across the sand. A crab's two front legs end in sharp claws called pincers.

A crab uses its pincers to catch and eat small sea animals.

Seagull

Seagulls keep their eggs safe by nesting in groups high up in the cliffs. Seagulls swoop down and dive into the sea for food.

A crab has a hard shell to protect its soft body.

Moving house

A hermit crab does not have a shell to protect its soft body.

It has to find the shell of a dead sea animal to live in.

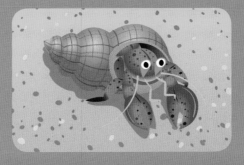

When it finds a shell that fits, the crab climbs in. Once this home is outgrown it will find another.

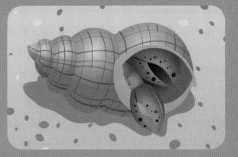

Seaweed

Seaweed is a sea plant. Green seaweed grows in shallow water. Brown seaweed usually grows in deeper water.

Fun at the beach

Beaches are really fun. You can build sandcastles, swim, paddle, and surf in the water, and have picnics by the water's edge.

Did you know?

Twice a day, at high tide, the sea level rises. At low tide the sea retreats back down the beach, leaving a line of seaweed and shells behind.

Cliff

Steep, rocky cliffs are found on coasts where crashing waves have worn away the land.

Tide pool

When the tide goes out on a rocky coast, pools of seawater are trapped in the rocks. These tide pools are home to all kinds of plants and animals.

surfer

tide pool

sea anemone

fish

mussels

Under the ocean

The world under the sea is filled with strange and beautiful creatures and plants. Some sea animals, like dolphins, swim near the surface of the water while others, like crabs, crawl along the seabed.

Fishing boat

Fishing boats use huge nets to catch thousands of fish at a time. Today, people are asked to be careful not to take too many fish so they don't die out.

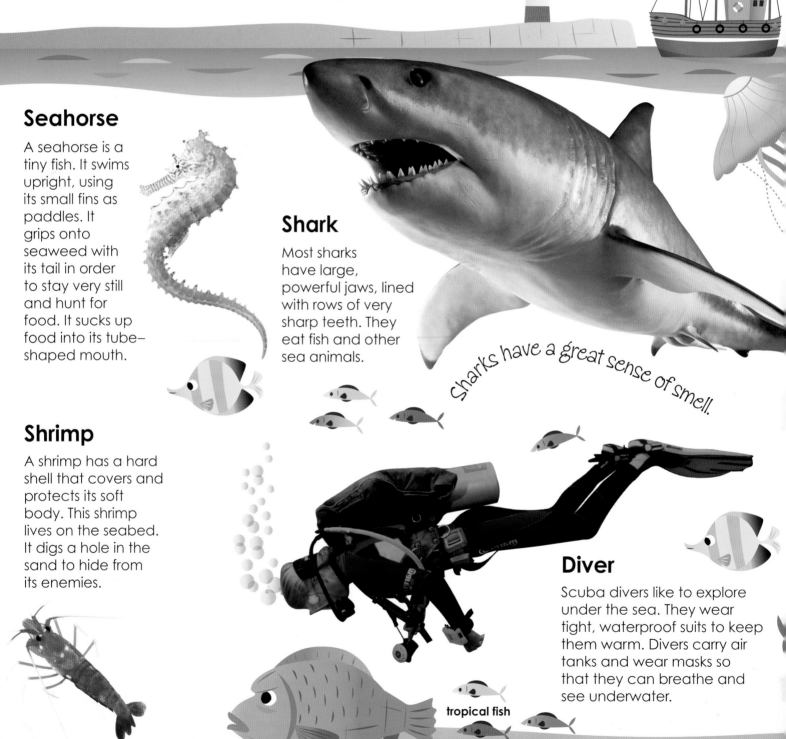

Seahorse

A seahorse is a tiny fish. It swims upright, using its small fins as paddles. It grips onto seaweed with its tail in order to stay very still and hunt for food. It sucks up food into its tube-shaped mouth.

Shark

Most sharks have large, powerful jaws, lined with rows of very sharp teeth. They eat fish and other sea animals.

Sharks have a great sense of smell.

Shrimp

A shrimp has a hard shell that covers and protects its soft body. This shrimp lives on the seabed. It digs a hole in the sand to hide from its enemies.

tropical fish

Diver

Scuba divers like to explore under the sea. They wear tight, waterproof suits to keep them warm. Divers carry air tanks and wear masks so that they can breathe and see underwater.

Dolphins can leap high above the water.

Dolphin

Dolphins are not fish—they are mammals. They live underwater but swim to the surface to breathe.

Plankton

Plankton is the name for tiny sea animals and plants. They are so small that they cannot be seen without a magnifying glass. Plankton is an important food for many sea creatures.

animal plankton

plant plankton

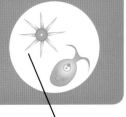

Plankton are much smaller than this in real life.

Octopus

An octopus has eight long tentacles covered with suckers. These help it walk and hold its prey. An octopus also uses its tentacles to feel and taste.

Tropical fish

These fish live in the warm, shallow waters of tropical coral reefs. They swim in large groups called shoals.

Jellyfish

A jellyfish uses its long tentacles to sting plankton or small fish. It then carries its prey to its mouth in the center of its soft body.

Coral reef

A coral reef takes thousands of years to form. It is built up from the skeletons of millions of tiny animals called coral polyps. A coral reef is home to all kinds of different sea creatures.

Shipwreck

Shipwrecks are fascinating places for divers to explore. They hunt for objects that sank with the ship and try to imagine what the ship was like before it was wrecked.

Did you know?

The Great Barrier Reef in Australia is the largest coral reef in the world. It is so big it can even be seen from space.

51

Space

Earth, where we live, is a planet surrounded by a layer of air called the atmosphere. Beyond the atmosphere is a vast space, containing the Sun, the Moon, and the other planets and stars. Astronauts travel to space in specially designed spacecraft to learn more about it.

The Sun

The Sun is a giant ball of very hot, glowing gases. Only a tiny part of its light (and heat) reaches us on Earth. But even this is so powerful that it can hurt your eyes if you look directly at it.

Solar system

The Earth is one of eight planets that move around the Sun in paths called orbits. The Sun and the eight planets are part of the solar system.

Starry sky

Look into the sky at night. Can you see that some bright stars make shapes in the sky? These groups of stars are called constellations. The one below is called "the big dipper."

Mercury **Venus** **Earth** **Mars**

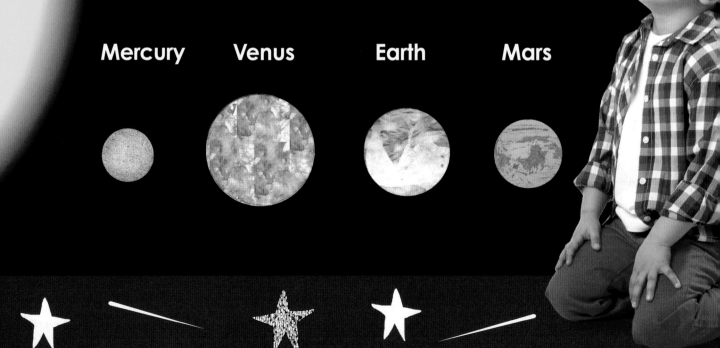

Moon landing

On July 20, 1969, two American astronauts, Neil Armstrong and Buzz Aldrin, became the first people to walk on the surface of the Moon. They traveled into space in the largest rocket that has ever been launched.

Weightlessness

When a spacecraft is in space, the people and things inside have no weight. They float in midair unless they are tied down. Astronauts sleep in special sleeping bags attached to the walls.

Did you know?

In space, liquids do not pour. Astronauts have to suck their drinks from special tubes otherwise the liquid floats around.

Did you know?

The "Great Red Spot" on Jupiter is the biggest storm in the known universe— the spot is at least three times the size of Earth.

Spacesuit

When astronauts leave their spacecraft they wear spacesuits. Big backpacks are built into the suits to carry the oxygen the astronauts need to breathe.

Jupiter

Saturn

Uranus

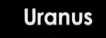

Neptune

Earth

Earth is a living planet. All kinds of plants, from trees to flowers, flourish on the land. Many animals live here too—lions and tigers roam on land, fish swim in the sea, and birds fly in the air. The landscape is varied too, with snow–capped mountains, deep valleys, dry deserts and lush, green rain forests.

A **globe** is a round model of our Earth.

Spinning Earth

The Earth takes about 365 days (one year) to travel around the Sun. As Earth travels, it spins like a top—rotating around the Sun, and this is why we have day and night.

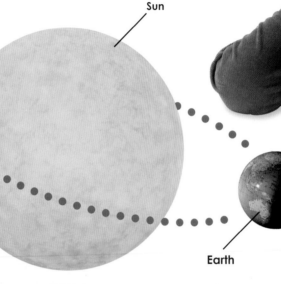

Sun

Earth

Inside the Earth

The Earth is made up of layers of rock. The surface is called the Earth's crust. If you could drill deep into the Earth's crust you would find pockets of hot, liquid rock, called magma. A volcano is caused when this hot liquid bursts through the surface.

Land, sea, air

Although it may come as a surprise, only one-third of the Earth is land. The rest is covered with water: seas, lakes, or rivers. Surrounding the Earth is the atmosphere.

Life on Earth

Earth was formed billions of years ago. Gradually, it started to change, and eventually life was formed. The very first creatures lived in the sea. Then came the dinosaurs—they were among the first reptiles. Today, there are all kinds of animals living on Earth.

Earth formed about 4,500 million years ago. Later came the dinosaurs!

Mapping it out

A map gives a flat picture of our round world, which is divided into seven main areas, called continents. This map shows each continent surrounded by the major oceans.

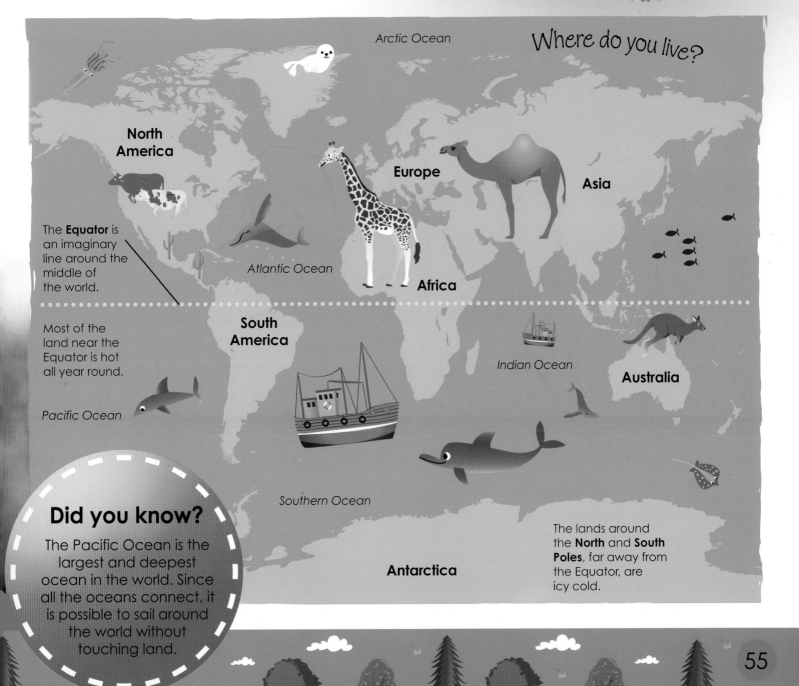

Arctic Ocean

Where do you live?

North America

Europe

Asia

The **Equator** is an imaginary line around the middle of the world.

Atlantic Ocean

Africa

Most of the land near the Equator is hot all year round.

South America

Indian Ocean

Australia

Pacific Ocean

Southern Ocean

Did you know?

The Pacific Ocean is the largest and deepest ocean in the world. Since all the oceans connect, it is possible to sail around the world without touching land.

Antarctica

The lands around the **North** and **South Poles**, far away from the Equator, are icy cold.

Seasons and weather

There are four seasons every year—spring, summer, fall, and winter. Each season brings changes in the weather. As the weather changes, the plants and animals begin to change too.

A rainbow appears when sunlight shines through a rain shower.

Spring

In spring, the world comes to life after the cold winter. The days grow longer and the weather gets warmer. Blossoms appear on some trees and many birds return from their winter homes.

Summer

Summer is the hottest season. There are leaves on the trees and the flowers bloom. People spend time outside, enjoying the long, sunny days.

Wind

Wind is moving air. Wind can be a light breeze or a strong gale. It is fun to fly a kite on a windy day.

Sun

The Sun gives out light and heat and its energy helps make the trees and plants grow. But it can be harmful, too. People need to protect their skin from its strong rays by using sun protection.

Rain boots and an umbrella keep us dry on splishy, splashy, rainy days!

Rain

The clouds in the sky are full of tiny drops of water. When the drops get too big and heavy, they fall to the ground as rain. There are often rain showers in the spring.

Fall

In fall, the wind gets colder and the days become shorter. Leaves fall off the trees. Some animals grow thicker fur to get ready for the cold winter.

Leaves

The leaves on some trees change color in different seasons. In spring, the leaves are pale green. In summer, they turn bright green, and in the fall, they turn orange, then brown, then they fall off the tree.

Winter

Winter is the coldest season of the year. Most trees are bare and many plants stop growing. People need to heat their homes and wear thicker clothes to keep warm. The freezing winds often bring snow and ice.

Snow

When the air is very cold, the drops of water in the clouds freeze. They turn into icy crystals that join up and fall to the ground as snowflakes. Snowflakes pile up into a layer of snow that covers the ground.

Storm

During a storm, dark clouds gather. There are loud bangs called thunder. Flashes of lightning light up the sky.

Did you know?

A tornado is a rotating column of air extending from a thunderstorm to the ground. The most dangerous ones can cause a lot of damage and swirl around at up to 300 mph (about 482 kmh).

Desert

A desert is a place where almost no rain falls. Only animals and plants that need very little water can live in a desert.

Scorpion

A scorpion has a nasty sting in its tail. It hunts at night, searching for insects to eat.

Sandy desert

Sandy deserts are covered in hills of shifting sand called dunes. Very few plants grow in these hot, dry lands.

palm tree   water well

An **oasis** is a place in the desert where water is found. People build a town around an oasis.

sand dune

Oil wells are drilled in some deserts to pump oil from deep under the ground.

Camel

A camel can survive for days without food or water. It lives on the fat stored in its hump. This camel is called a dromedary and has one hump. It lives in the deserts of Africa, the Middle East, and Australia.

A camel's thick eyelashes protect its eyes from sand blown by the wind.

Two-humped camel

This Bactrian camel has two humps on its back. It lives in Asia where the desert is cooler.

meerkat

Rocky desert

In some deserts the land is rocky and bare. Plants that store their own water, like cacti, grow in the dry, rocky deserts of North America.

Rattlesnake

A rattlesnake gets its name from the rattle on the end of its tail. It shakes its tail from side to side to warn other animals to stay away.

Beetle

This beetle has yellowish wing cases that makes it hard to see on the desert sand. Its long legs hold its body off the hot ground.

Lizard

This desert lizard has sharp spines on its back. These spines protect it from attack.

Did you know?

Rattlesnakes feed on mice, rabbits, and other small animals. They stun their prey with their deadly bite and swallow them whole.

This **rattlesnake** buries itself in the sand to keep cool during the very hot days.

Elf owls nest in holes in this tall cactus plant.

Cactus

A Saguaro cactus grows very slowly. It can live for up to 200 years and grow taller than a house.

Strong, dry winds blow across the desert plains and carve the **rocks** into strange shapes.

Tuareg people

The Tuareg people of Africa live in goatskin tents in the Sahara desert. They are nomads, moving from place to place to find grass for their camels and goats. Tuareg people use camels to carry their belongings across the desert.

Tuareg people hang their belongings in trees to keep them safe from animals.

Grasslands

Grasslands are flat plains where grass, low bushes, and few trees grow. The weather is hot and dry for much of the year, but some grasslands have a rainy season. The grasslands are home to many different animals, from plant-eating elephants and zebras, to meat-eating animals like lions.

Vulture

Vultures use their excellent eyesight to spot prey from high above the grasslands. They do not kill their own food but scavenge dead carcases from other animals.

Zebra

Zebras live in large groups called herds. While the rest of the herd grazes, the leaders watch out for danger.

Did you know?

Elephants can swim underwater for up to six hours by using their trunk as a snorkel.

African savannah

The hottest areas of grasslands are called savannah. The African savannah is one of the last places left in the world where there are still large herds of wild animals. Hundreds of animals gather at water holes to drink.

A **giraffe's** long legs and neck help it reach the leaves at the tops of tall trees.

A **hippo** keeps cool by lying in a water hole with just its eyes, nose, and ears showing above the surface.

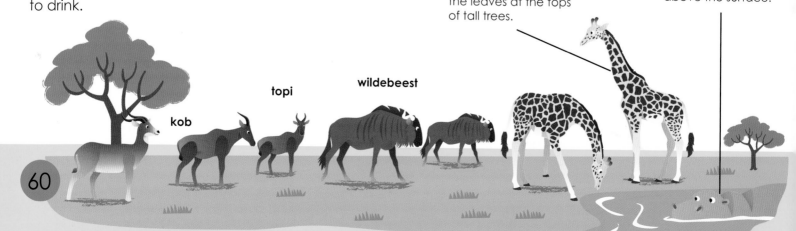

kob

topi

wildebeest

Xhosa people

Many Xhosa people live in villages on the grasslands of southern Africa. They live in beehive-shaped houses, which they build themselves. Living in these barren lands can be hard and sometimes the men, or whole families, have to move to cities to find work.

Many Xhosa women look after the crops in the village.

Children take care of the cattle. They move them around to find fresh grass.

Elephant

The African elephant is the biggest animal on land. The elephant's nose and upper lip form a long, supple trunk. It uses its trunk like a hand to pick plants and put them into its mouth, to smell and to drink.

Lion

Lions lie in wait at watering holes to pounce on animals that come to drink. They spend the rest of their time asleep in the shade.

Australian grasslands

Animals like kangaroos, wallabies, and dingoes live on the hot, dry plains of central Australia. Tall eucalyptus trees grow on the banks of rivers and creeks and are home to flocks of brightly colored birds.

Dingoes are a type of wild dog. They hunt together in groups called packs.

Emus are the second largest birds in the world. They cannot fly, but they run very fast on flat ground.

Kangaroo

A kangaroo uses its long tail to balance as it leaps over the ground. A baby kangaroo, called a joey, is carried in a special pouch on its mother's belly.

Rain forest

Rain forests grow in hot and rainy parts of the world. Millions of animals live among the thick undergrowth and tall trees. Some live high up in the treetops, where they can see the sun. Here, the leaves and plants make a kind of roof called a canopy.

Did you know?

The longest known snake is the reticulated python. It can grow up to 30 ft (about 9 m) long!

Butterfly

These butterflies live in the canopy of the rain forest. Their colorful wings make them easy to spot as they fly through shafts of sunlight.

Hummingbird

This tiny bird beats its wings so fast that they make a humming sound. Hummingbirds hover in the air and sip sweet juice, called nectar, from flowers.

Tree frog

This tiny frog lives in the forest canopy. It grips the leaves with its sticky fingers and toes.

Rain forest plant

This plant grows on the forest floor and has the largest flowers in the world. It gives off a smell of rotting meat to attract flies.

Jaguar

A jaguar is a big wild cat. It can climb trees and swim. The jaguar's spotted coat makes it difficult to see as it stalks through the shady rain forest.

A hummingbird uses its long beak to reach deep inside flowers.

Snake

This snake is called a python. It eats small animals and birds. The python climbs trees by coiling itself around branches.

Yanomami people

Some Yanomami people still follow a traditional way of life in remote parts of the rain forest in South America. They hunt animals and birds, gather food like berries and fruit from the forest, and plant crops in small clearings.

A Yanomami man shows a young child how to plant seeds, using a special digging tool.

Monkey

There are many kinds of monkey living in the rain forest. This monkey uses its strong arms and legs to jump from branch to branch.

Sloth

A sloth moves very slowly. It spends most of its life upside down in trees. The sloth grips the branches with its long, hooked claws.

Chameleon

Chameleons catch their prey by sitting very quietly until an insect passes by. Then the chameleon shoots out its long, sticky tongue and pulls the insect back into its mouth.

Mountains

Mountain tops are bare and rocky, and often covered in snow. At the top, the air is very cold, so few plants can grow. Animals that can fly or climb, like eagles and goats, live high up in the mountains. On the lower slopes there are often thick forests, which are home to animals like bears and wild cats.

A **waterfall** forms when the snow at the top of a mountain melts and the stream of water drops down a steep rock face.

Eagles make their nests high up on the mountainside where their eggs will be safe.

Mountaineer

Some people climb mountains as a sport. They use ropes and picks to help them climb the steep rocks.

Wild cat

Wild cats live in the thick forest on some mountain slopes. They prowl at night, hunting small animals to eat. A wild cat's thick fur keeps it warm in the cold mountain air.

rope

backpac

water bot

Mountaineers wear **helmets** to protect their heads from falling stones.

hiking boots

Chamois

A chamois is a mountain goat. It has soft pads on its hooves to help it grip as it climbs up steep, rocky mountains.

Spectacular mountains

Rocky Mountains

Located in the western part of North America, the highest peak of this range is Mount Elbert—14,440 ft (about 4,401 m) above sea level.

The Andes

This is the longest mountain range in the world. It is a continual stretch of highland running along the western coast of South America.

The Himalayas

The Himalayan mountain range in Asia has some of the highest mountain peaks in the world, including the gigantic Mount Everest.

Bear

The huge, brown grizzly bear lives in the mountains of North America. It eats almost anything—from plants, fruit, and berries, to honey, fish, and meat.

A grizzly bear uses its humped shoulders and sharp, hooked claws to dig for food.

Skier

Humans have been using skis for transportation for thousands of years, but now skiing is also a popular mountain sport.

Ski lifts or **cable cars** carry skiers high up the mountainside so that they can ski down the smooth ski slopes.

Skiers wear warm, waterproof clothing and thick boots to help them stay dry and warm.

Ski poles have rings on the ends to keep them from sinking into the soft snow.

Cold lands

The cold regions near the North and South Poles are covered in ice and snow for most of the year. Few animals and even fewer plants can live in these areas. Animals like polar bears and huskies have thick fur to keep them warm.

Seal

This seal lives in the Arctic. It swims fast, using its flippers. A thick layer of fat under the seal's skin helps keep it warm in the icy water.

Polar bear

Polar bears hunt for food on the arctic snowfields near the North Pole. They catch seals and fish through holes in the ice. Polar bears use their large, sharp claws to catch and kill their prey.

Did you know?

Polar bears are so well padded with fat and thick fur that they can quickly overheat, even when it's freezing. They walk slowly and spend a lot of time resting to avoid this.

Penguin

Penguins live in Antarctica. They cannot fly, but are fast underwater swimmers. They use their short wings as flippers to speed through the water. Penguins spend most of their lives in the sea, but nest and feed their chicks on land.

Inuit people

Inuit people live in the Arctic regions of North America, Greenland, and Russia. Some Inuit people still live by hunting and fishing as they have done for thousands of years.

Husky

A husky is a large dog with a thick, shaggy coat. People who travel near the North Pole use teams of huskies to pull their sleds across the snow.

Life in Antarctica

The only people who live near the South Pole in Antarctica are explorers or scientists. They study the whales, birds, fish, and other animals that live in the area.

Northern Lights

At the North Pole, beautiful lights can be seen glowing in the night sky at particular times of the year. They are called the Northern Lights.

Icebreaker ships plow through the frozen seas to open a path for other boats.

Research stations in the Antarctic have powerful radios. The people who work there use the radios to keep in contact with the rest of the world.

Iceberg

An iceberg is a huge piece of ice that floats in the sea. Most of the iceberg lies beneath the surface of the water.

Killer whales swim together in groups called pods. They hunt seals, penguins, and squid to eat.

Whale

Many kinds of whales live in the seas around the North and South Poles. A whale swims under water, but comes up to the surface to breathe. It blows stale air out of the blowhole on the top of its head.

Did you know?

Summer days in the Arctic are very long. It is only dark for a few hours each night. In the middle of the summer the sun doesn't set at all and there's no night.

On land

Most people travel on land along roads. Cars, trucks, buses, and motorcycles speed along, carrying passengers and goods from one place to another. People who need to travel long distances often use wide roads called highways.

Riding a bike instead of using a car means less pollution in the air.

Car

Many people today travel around in a car. Most cars have four wheels and an engine that runs on gas or diesel fuel.

Tram

A tram runs on rails. It carries lots of passengers and can climb up steep hills. Some trams have wires that give them electricity to move.

Off-road vehicle

An off-road vehicle is specially built for driving over soft sand or rough ground. It has a powerful engine and wide, ridged tires that grip the ground.

Bicycle

A bicycle has two wheels that the rider turns by pushing on the pedals. Racing bicycles are light with narrow tires so that they can go fast. A mountain bike has wider tires and can be ridden over rough paths and tracks.

Did you know?

One of the first gasoline-powered vehicles was the Reitwagen—a motorized bicycle with a pair of stabilizers—built in Germany in 1885.

Motorcycle

A motorcycle has two wheels like a bicycle, but is powered by an engine. Motorcycles can move quickly through heavy traffic.

Truck

Trucks are big vehicles with powerful engines. They can carry heavy loads over long distances. Some trucks have tanks for carrying liquids, and others are refrigerated to keep the food they carry fresh.

Cart and horses

Some people travel in carts or carriages pulled by horses, oxen, or donkeys. Others ride horses to get from place to place.

Bus

A bus carries lots of people at a time. Some buses carry school children, others carry people around town, and still others take people on long trips.

Traffic

Heavy traffic gives off fumes that make the air dirty. This pollution makes it difficult for plants to grow and for people and other animals to breathe.

Train

Traveling by train is quick and safe. Passengers sit in cars, which are pulled or pushed along the rails by an engine. Trains that travel overnight have beds in them and are called sleeper trains.

On water

People have invented hundreds of different ways of traveling on water. Big ships and boats carry people and heavy loads long distances far out to sea, while smaller boats, like sailboats, can be sailed on lakes and rivers.

Sailboat

Sailboats, like powerboats, are recreational boats that people ride on for fun or in races as a sport. Sailboats move by the wind blowing into their sails. Racing sailboats are light so they can move through water at high speeds.

This small **sailboat** can be sailed by one or two people. Larger boats have more crew members.

A **lighthouse** warns ships that they are close to shore.

Huge **container ships** and oil tankers off-load their cargo into waiting trucks.

Floating market

In some parts of the world goods are transported up and down rivers and sold out of boats. Floating markets attract tourists with colorful food displays.

Harbor

A harbor is built in a sheltered place on the coast. Ships and boats can safely drop anchor or dock and load and unload their goods and passengers. Tugboats help large ships steer in and out of the harbor.

Hovercraft

A hovercraft can move over both land and sea on a huge cushion of air. A hovercraft carries passengers on short sea journeys. Big propellers push the hovercraft forward.

Submarine

Submarines are boats that are often used for exploring under the water, sometimes for months at a time.

Did you know?

The first ship to complete an underwater voyage to the North Pole was USS Nautilus in 1958.

Speedboat

A speedboat is a small boat with a powerful engine. Its sleek, pointed shape helps it speed over the water. Speedboats are often used for racing and for sports like water–skiing.

Paddle steamer

Paddle steamers were first built over 100 years ago. A steam engine turns a big wheel that moves the boat forward.

Cruise ship

Cruise ships, also called liners, carry hundreds of passengers on vacations. Cruise ships are like floating hotels, with stores, bars, swimming pools, and hundreds of rooms, or cabins, for people to sleep in.

A porthole is a ship's round window.

On every ship there are small boats called **lifeboats**. These are used to rescue passengers if the ship gets in trouble.

By air

For hundreds of years people tried to fly. At first, they copied the birds by tying wings to their arms, but they always crashed. About 100 years ago, the first airplane took off into the sky. Now, people travel long distances in airplanes and other air transportation every day.

Glider

This is a glider. It has no engine. Another plane tows it into the sky with a cable. When the cable is released, the glider soars through the air.

Hot–air balloon

Hot–air balloons are shaped like huge paper bags. A burner fills the bag (or balloon) with warm air to keep it afloat once it is in the air.

Helicopters are often used for rescuing people in danger.

Helicopter

The blades whirl around, lifting the helicopter into the air.

A helicopter has four blades instead of wings. It can fly straight upward and hover in the air. This means that a helicopter can take off and land almost anywhere.

Seaplane

A seaplane can land on water. It has two floats instead of wheels. Seaplanes are used in places where there is no room for a runway on the land.

Did you know?

The first aircraft to carry passengers was a hot-air balloon. On board were a sheep, a chicken, and a duck.

Light aircraft

A light aircraft is a small plane. It carries only a few people and can land on short runways. In large countries some people use light aircraft instead of cars to travel long distances.

Flight crew

The pilot and co-pilot are called flight crew. They sit in the cockpit and fly the plane, using instruments to make sure that the plane travels at the right speed and height.

Passenger plane

This huge airplane is called a jumbo jet. It carries up to 500 passengers at a time and flies long distances all over the world.

cockpit

cargo hold

Four powerful **jet engines** are fixed under the jumbo's wings.

An airplane flight

Boarding
After handing in tickets at the check-in desk, and completing a security check, passengers can board the airplane. Large bags are stowed in the cargo hold.

Take off
The plane speeds down the runway until it lifts off the ground. Once the plane is safely in the sky passengers can remove their seatbelts and move around.

In flight
Once in the air, flight attendants help make the trip comfortable by providing passengers with refreshments. Sometimes they are shown a movie.

Index